SUPERVISORY

MANAGEMENT

Table of Contents

INTRODUCTION TO SUPERVISORY MANAGEMENT

A manager or supervisor is someone who has the responsibility of overseeing the day to day activities in an organization. A manager/ supervisor can have one person to a thousand people working under him.

Managers have different leadership styles from the Autocratic – who makes unilateral decisions and does not seek input from subordinates to the Paternalistic – who makes decisions but has the best interest of the employees at heart to the Democratic - who involves everyone in decision making to the Laissez faire – who just takes a back seat and let employees or subordinates make their own decisions.

The concept of supervisory management evolved as more and more companies reached new development levels, requiring specialized personnel to oversee and manage employees from different fields of activity. Today, there are a lot of people who work as supervisors in a company, taking advantage of their own abilities in order to effectively manage the employees under their care. The supervisor is the one that puts the whole team dynamics into motion, making sure that the workplace functions smoothly and that no problems arise.

3

In many ways, the supervisor can be compared to a manager. Some people consider the activity of supervisory management to be just as important as the overall management of a company. The supervisor occupies a position of high importance within a company, as the general manager puts a lot of trust in that person for the success of the business. Supervisory management means having both the power and the authority to handle the dynamics of the workplace; the supervisor coordinates the activity of the employees of a company, without actually intervening in their daily work.

The idea behind supervisory management is that employees receive instructions on how to perform their work. Once they receive these instructions or orders from the supervisor, the wheels are in motion. The whole office/department dynamics depend on the professionalism and dedication of the supervisor; if he knows how to spread his/her authority, then it is guaranteed that the workplace will function smoothly. The authority matter is serious, because the supervisor can be held accountable for everything that the employee does wrong. This is not strictly related to the work activity but also to the actions of the employee in general; once again, there are specific supervisory management techniques that a professional supervisor will use in his line of work.

We have talked about power and authority. These are two of the most important attributes when it comes to supervisory management. However, there is one more thing to be taken into account. That is responsibility. When the supervisor has a team of employees to oversee, that person is responsible for everything related to that work force. He/she needs to make sure that the team produces or delivers the expected services, within the timeframe requested and also matching the highest standards of quality. While every employee is responsible on his own for the things mentioned above, it is the main job of the supervisor to oversee all of them. That comes with a huge level of responsibility, especially one takes into account the costs involved with damage control and safety strategy implementation.

While the supervisory management involves being held accountable for the productivity and actions of the employees, it should not be confused with general management. The supervisor is often compared to the manager but these are actually two different job positions. In order to clarify such matters, it should be mentioned that the supervisor does not hold the authority to hire new employees, nor to terminate the contract of existing ones. Moreover, supervisory management is not related to budget control, as this is usually handled by the general manager.

Returning to the hiring of new employees, it is important to mention that the human resources department is actually the one that handles such matters. This does not mean that the supervisor cannot take part in the hiring process. He/she has complete liberty to participate in the process but, as part of the supervisory management department, cannot make any final decisions. Another important aspect is related to the termination of a contract. If a supervisor has reason to recommend that a certain employee be fired, he/she has the liberty to do that. The recommendation, however, may or may not be taken into account by the general manager.

Apart from handling team dynamics, supervisory management may sometimes be connected with other aspects. For example, the supervisor might decide to use part of the budget in order to make certain acquisitions. The spending limit will be decided by the financial department and approved by the general manager. Apart from that, the supervisor will be instructed to decide on the work time frame for each employee and also handle any issues related to the payment of the said employees. The diversity of work is what makes the field of supervisory management so exciting.

Supervisory management should not be viewed as a one way street. Given the fact that the supervisor comes in contact on a daily basis with the employees, we should also take into account the reverse team dynamics. This means that the supervisor will also have to handle employees coming to him/her; the employee will want to have his needs and problems taken care of. Supervisory management does not include only giving instructions to employees and making sure that they follow them; it also means ensuring the satisfaction of the employee at the workplace.

For many companies, the supervisory management department acts as the connection between the general management and the actual employees. The supervisor handles many manager-like tasks and that leaves the general manager with plenty of time to handle more important matters. As for the supervisor, he will handle new tasks on a regular basis, depending on the company. Some companies require the supervisory management department to handle the training of the employees or the implementation of the safety working strategies. Others impose their supervisors to handle everything that is related to the workforce, no matter the previous experience.

Someone once said that a good supervisor is the kind of person who can recognize a problem straight ahead and already figure out a solution when it happens. Analyzing the field of supervisory management, it is safe to say that visualizing the problem and finding the solution is not enough. The supervisor has to visualize the opportunities presented in the work field as well, not to mention carry out the policies of the company and organize the work force. As companies step into the new generation, the field of supervisory management evolves, showing a new dynamics of the work team.

UNIT2

COMMUNICATION

Stepping into the role of a supervisor or manager is a great achievement. Although it does come with great responsibility to oversee, supervise and manage the team that is under you. To work well with your team to enhance overall productivity and profit, it is important to communicate appropriately to make sure everyone knows what they are doing, what is expected of them, and how you can improve workplace behaviour. For a supervisor or manager there are many ways you can communicate with your team without causing friction or mis-interpretation. These strategies include:

Use Constructive Criticism

Constructive criticism is a special form of criticism which uses both positive and negative comments that offer well-reasoned and valid opinions in a friendly manner towards a working situation or problem. The purpose of this type of criticism is to help with improving the overall outcome of the job or project. With teams, constructive criticism can become a valuable tool to help with maintaining and raising performance standards. For this criticism to work, it is important to always focus on the work and not on the actual person or team that is hired. Where possible any personality issues should be avoided. This type of criticism is most likely to be used by a team if it is detailed, specific, clear, timely, and most of all actionable.

Be Personal

Getting to know your team is also essential to not only open a better line of communication but to also give you the ability to interact and work better with the team to get results. Interact with each person on the team. This will show them that they are not just "work horses" in the workplace and will make them feel like they are a part of the team. Other options include using first name basis, as well as sharing any concerns, excitement or ideas they may have in a professional and friendly way.

Listen To The Team And Their Feedback

A team is designed to work together and communicate different ideas until a solution to a problem is resolved. It is important for any manager or supervisor overseeing the team to always listen to input the team has to offer, and any feedback that they may have to suggestions from you or other team members. Remember that the job you are supervising is a team effort and should be conducted in this manner. Managers who listen to their team are more likely to get better results overall.

Always Recognize Team Member

Recognition or a lack of it, can directly impact the level of engagement a team member offers when problem solving. Team members who feel undervalued or unrecognized are one of the reasons why a team member may leave, or the team may falter in getting the results needed to solve a problem in a timely fashion. When discussing a problem with your team, take note of any of the members who may not be speaking up or who may look as if they are feeling left out. For team members such as this, engage with them by asking them if they have any input, feedback or solutions. Always take their input in a positive way, even if it may not be as useful as needed at the time. Showing your interest and recognising all team members as individuals with different ideas will help to create a stronger line of communication.

Always Show Positivity

Showing positivity, even in a tough situation, is also another important way a supervisor or manager can communicate with the team. Positivity and hope has shown to boost team moral and can lead to a much more engaged workforce. With any negative problem or situation, try to always offer a positive solution with a positive attitude. This will not only help to communicate your ideas and opinions to the team but will also help to elevate some of the negative tension that some team members may be feeling.

Act On Your Word

Any type of communication will directly impact the team, this includes nonverbal communication. To help you maintain respect, team trust, and credibility as a supervisor or manager through any honest and open communication you have conducted in the past, it important to back up any of your words with action. For example, if you have promised to make a change to some of your teams working environment, or if you have said about implementing a new course of action to a certain problem, it is important to keep to your word and do it. Once you have turned your words into action, communicate this with your team.

Be Respectful To Your Team Members

Being a supervisor or manager doesn't mean you have the right to be disrespectful to those under your supervision. When communicating with your team members never judge them, ridicule them, or speak to them in a negative way that may cause them to feel like they may be inadequate at the job at hand. Respectful communication between managers and their team will help to keep team member moral and confidence high without causing any additional stress, self-doubt or self-confidence issues throughout the team workplace. By respecting your team members, you will also be treated with respect and will have more chance of having a well-functioning and successful team environment.

Be Open and Honest

A supervisor or manager should also communicate to their team with openness and honesty at all times. This can be hard when a conflict arises, although by being honest and open about a situation whilst using constructive criticism can help to bridge the gap in communication that may have become damaged. Being open and honest will also allow you to maintain your credibility, team trust, and respect. Remember when being honest to your team, try to speak in a non-condescending manner. Always be respectful, polite, and straightforward whilst communicating.

Overall

Communication is one of the most powerful tools any supervisor or manager has to offer in a workplace team environment. Effective supervisor-team communication can help to increase the overall team engagement in problem solving, as well as boost productivity in the workplace, and drive business success.

UNIT 3

MOTIVATION

To win the loyalty of their customers, businesses must start by winning the confidence of their workers. Companies rely on the effectiveness of their managers – who link upper management to the rest of the organization – to foster business growth. As a result, supervisors have to devise ways of tapping into the morale of their team members to encourage accomplishment of work goals.

Employees usually blame supervisors for their lack of motivation. However simply being good at one's job doesn't cut it. This unit covers how a supervisor or manager could boost the morale of his team members, and it explains why motivation is important when it comes to organizational teamwork.

How to Encourage Teamwork

In most organizational settings, change is perceived in a negative light, which is why making time to communicate and build strong bonds is the best approach to boost employee confidence. Employees become more motivated and committed when their leaders share their goals, vision, and optimism. The following motivational tips boost teamwork among employees.

Regular communication

Communication creates an inclusive environment which motivates employees. Regular communication equips employees with the information they need to execute their duties. In addition, it makes them feel recognized, important, and binds the workers with their superiors and with the organization, in general.

Clear, transparent, and genuine communication is essential. Whether a supervisor is busy or not, he has to make time for his team: by taking them to lunch, taking office rounds in the afternoons, or just making time to talk to each member of his team regularly. Not doing so drifts them apart.

Convey leadership's sanguinity

By helping employees understand how leadership thinks – its sanguinity and vision – the supervisor eliminates pessimism. Team members begin to act and think in a manner that drives results. When people start believing that they could succeed, they become self-motivated and work more aggressively towards their goals. As a result, supervisors must seek every opportunity they get to convey their optimism to their team members – through all they say and do.

Share the vision

Optimism inspires people to be their best, but is has to be coupled with vision. By telling team members where the organization was, where it is currently, and where it is heading, they get something to look forward to. When the supervisor share's the organization's plan for a better and brighter future, the action it must take, and constantly remind his team members the reasons that will make them successful, their spirit of teamwork becomes rejuvenated.

Build healthy relationships

Real motivation lies behind trust. When the presence of leadership is felt among employees, they feel at ease and more willing to follow its vision. Relationships help supervisors know their team members better, that is, how they can motivate them, coach them, and lead them more effectively. In addition, bonds help team members know their supervisor as well. In essence, the best motivators are those who have a good relationship with their teammates.

Create purpose within the team

Purpose pushes people to a level that is beyond their comprehension. The desire to make a difference makes people go the extra mile to achieve their goals. Sitting down with each employee, trying to understand their personal goals, and then integrating them into the organization's vision intensifies their urge to take action. By creating purpose-driven goals, supervisors tap into the morale of their team members by making them feel that what they are doing is positively contributing to the general success of the company and the world as a whole.

Care for the team

All employees like feeling valued. When team members believe that you care for them, they will invest their highest potential in their work. Supervisors who make time to invest in their teams gain creativity, productivity, and loyalty. Care is the greatest motivator of all.

Why Motivation is Important

Motivation encourages action. Every goal has a financial, physical, and human resource aspect. Through motivation, the human resource aspect can be fully utilized. Creating willingness on the part of the employee helps a business secure the best possible exploitation of resources.

It increases efficiency. Qualifications and abilities play a major role when it comes to appointing employees to certain positions. However, performance is dependent on filling the gap between one's ability and his willingness to work. Motivation not only helps fill the gap, it also enables employees to increase their output, to reduce operational costs, and generally improve efficiency.

Helps organizations achieve their goals. Organizations usually concentrate their efforts on adequate utilization of resources, creation of a collective work environment, and the creation of purpose-driven objectives to reach a common goal(s). Motivation enables supervisors and employees to work together to achieve collective organizational objectives.

It builds strong bonds. Action, that promote enthusiasm among employees, does not need to be expensive. In fact, company financed events have a short-term effect compared to how employees are treated in their workplace every day. Factors such as attention from supervisors, employee-oriented policies, and genuine care go a long way toward appreciating and valuing team members and fostering healthy relationships.

It helps reveal a clear sense of direction. The best leaders are the ones who come up with clear frameworks that outline expected performance. When employees know what is expected of them, they act in a manner that is consistent with their organization's expectations.

It creates an environment in which employees feel inspired to work. However, an inspirational environment is not enough; supervisors must also consider factors such as creating a bottom line, criticizing worker performance, and measure success.

It stabilizes the workforce. Employees, who enjoy working for their organization, will talk about their great experience with their friends. Consequently, the venture will gain a good reputation with time. When a vacancy becomes available, it will attract the best and the brightest employees due to the excellent reputation that the organization has.

Conclusion

To achieve success, supervisors must believe in their teams' ability to achieve success. Not believing in something leads to inaction. When directors genuinely believe that their organizations can achieve success, they transfer their belief to their team members. This fuels action and produces the desired results.

UNIT 4

DELEGATING

The practice of turning over work or tasks to the subordinates by the senior management in a business is known as delegation. Among the many factors that make management successful, delegation is one of them. This is because it not only gets the staff to do the work but it also assures them that their boss trust them. Delegation therefore is a very powerful motivational tool that can be used by every manger that needs his or her employers to become better at what they do.

How to Delegate in Order to Increase the Performance of Employees

Delegation gives the employees enough freedom, authority and responsibility to meet any company's set goals. There are many ways that management can decide to carry out delegation in an organization. When delegating, the manager has to pick the right person to delegate the tasks to. It is important that before assigning a particular task to an employee, you carefully examine their skills and knowledge on the task in question. This ensures that each person is assigned a task they will fully commit to and achieve within a set time, using the available resources.

At times, work can delegated to one person. This is usually done to help improve the chosen individual's performance, increase his or her production level or make them more focused on achieving the set goals. Once you delegate work, it is necessary that you ask the person who has been assigned the job to provide you with their work progress. However, you should always remember that you have only delegated the work but not shown how it should be done. When delegating, you are simply telling the employee that you trust their capabilities. As a result, they should come up with the most effective way of achieving the given task.

When delegating work, you need to clearly indicate the expected results for the task in question. You can mention all those who should be involved in achieving the task, how and where to get the resources and any other necessary information. While the employee undertakes the task, ensure you maintain an open communication process. This will make it easy for the person to report to you on the progress made as well as seek assistance if they need any.

There is always the chance you will not be satisfied with the results of the project. In such a situation, you should not try to do the task yourself because this will make the involved employee feel unmotivated. Try to reason things out together with the person and offer any assistance they might need in perfecting their work. Also, do not forget to congratulate them for the work done. This helps to motivate them and they become more focused in offering better services.

Benefits of Delegation

The following are some of the main benefits of delegation.

Increased work quality

When employees are given full responsibility over their specified tasks within the organization, they get a chance to better understand the products and services offered by the company. This in turn increases their performance. It also makes them feel motivated due to the fact that the management is entrusting them with certain tasks. This will make them work even harder to maintain that trust.

Improves the organizational flow of authority

Delegation acts as a ground on which the superior-subordinate relationship stands. The top management delegates tasks to the subordinates and this helps to ensure that all the set goals of the organization are achieved.

Offer personal benefits to the managers

The managerial tasks are normally very hectic and managers barely have time to deal with their personal issues. Through delegation, managers can get time to do other activities as they assign tasks to their subordinates. Through delegation, they can also get time to focus more on controlling and planning of company issues.

Improve the skills of their subordinates

By delegating tasks to subordinates, you give them full responsibility and freedom to apply their knowledge in achieving a certain task. Since you are not controlling them, they feel a sense of pride and will therefore do their best to ensure that the task is achieved. This, in turn, would improve their skills and knowledge, and they also come up with new ways of achieving certain objectives. With delegation, the organization will have more effective decision makers.

Monitoring work progress and achievements

Subordinates will do their best to ensure that work assigned to them flows smoothly. They will feel the need to provide you with the daily performance or progress of the job they are doing. This would give you a chance to concentrate on other matters while still keeping track of what is going on in the company.

Creation of work teams with desired skills and knowledge about a certain task

People's knowledge and skills regarding different tasks tend to vary depending on the individual. While you delegate, you could create teams based on an individuals' skills and knowledge in certain areas. It is actually through delegation that you can create strong teams in your organization, each one of them depending on the capabilities you discover in every employee.

Motivation tool

As the teams submit their daily performance reports, take the opportunity to congratulate them on a job well done. This would motivate them to become better employees. You could also use this opportunity to reward their good work and offer guidance where they seem stuck.

In order to achieve the benefits discussed above, management should ensure that work is delegated properly. There are very serious damages that can be caused by improper delegation. For instance it could affect the overall production of the company, or lead to poor completion of tasks, which could affect the entire company. It is therefore advisable that managers ensure they delegate the right work to the right people. In addition, managers should also be readily available to offer guidance to their subordinates. The truth is that delegation could be very successful and helpful in improving a company's production if management delegates carefully.

UNIT 5

CONFLICT RESOLUTION

An organization, specifically a workplace, is made up of different kinds of people. People of different qualifications and abilities come together with an aim of achieving organizational goals. Nevertheless, there comes a time when someone might have his/her personal needs or thoughts, which might differ from other employees. In such a case, there might be an occurrence of a conflict. Conflicts in a workplace are prone to happen.

Mostly, the existence of a conflict in an organization will affect the productivity, and there will be frustration in the workplace. There could be a group of people, who are the major causes of conflicts in an organization. This tends to add more work, which was not assigned by the management, to other workers. One fact about a conflict is that it cannot naturally go away, and it will get deeper whenever it is ignored.

There are several types of conflicts that are common in nearly every organization. Some are easy to identify, while others might require keen observation. Some of the common identifiers of conflicts include the following:

- Negative attitude. This one is a small, event that can be easily identified. It can end up causing people to strike.
- Low productivity. It might not be easy to detect that the production level has decreased. This would take a while to detect.

These two events involve the affected morale of the worker, which is most likely caused by the existence of a conflict.

Policies Of Conflict Resolution

There are some conflicts that would need the manager to intervene, while in most cases, most of the conflict will need the workers to solve the issues themselves. Here are some policies that can help the teams to solve their conflicts at the workplace.

1. Understanding The Situation

One thing that causes people to have conflicts is the misunderstanding between the two. Mostly, a situation might occur, which would be the main cause of a conflict. For that reason, before one can start to resolve a conflict, they must understand the situation. Understanding the situation also helps people to know how to develop the resolution of the conflict.

2. Recognize The Issue/Problem

When you have understood the situation that caused the conflict, you will then need to acknowledge the problem. One board member might want the company to flow in one direction, while another would oppose the suggestion. The employees can also have issues between them, which would end up causing a conflict. Knowing the problem itself, and clearly understanding it is a great step in conflict resolution. When the problem has been recognized, it will help the workers to approach it directly.

3. Take Your Time. Be Patient

Here, it will need the workers to take time in responding to the conflict. Usually, when one is frustrated, they will most likely make irrational decisions. For that, when people in a workplace are having a conflict, they would make decisions that are not reasonable enough. The most common reason of the decision they make is because they want to be better than the people they are in conflict with. For that reason, always ensure that you have taken your time well. Being patient helps you make rational decisions.

4. Avoid Intimidation And Force

Usually, when you try to coerce some people into following the way that you want, they might only follow it for some time. Nevertheless, this will only be for a short time, and there are higher odds for the problem to reoccur. It is discouraged be intimidating, especially during conflicts. This only tends to cause more problems in the future. It is important to be kind, and allow people to make decisions that are comfortable with them. Mostly, it is recommended to come up with an understanding with the persons whom you have a conflict with.

5. Look At The Problem, And Not The Person

In many situations, a workplace will always have one problematic person. In most cases, the person is always perceived to be the major cause of conflicts. This might be common in many organizations, but it is very unhealthy for the given organization. The habit of pointing fingers to specific people only causes more conflicts. The people would feel discouraged in doing their work well. Instead, you should focus on the problem itself. For instance, if a person was supposed to send emails to clients, and they are late to do so, do not look at the one who was supposed to do it. Instead, you should look at how the emails should be sent to the clients as soon as possible. Focusing on the problem helps to enlighten people on what they should have done.

6. Develop Rules

Prior to carrying out an official meeting with the people who have conflicts, you should establish guidelines that will help to maintain order during the meeting. You should establish the rules that will make them be calm when expressing themselves. This will help to maintain discipline during the meeting. You can also include that any violation of the rules would lead to the termination of the meeting.

7. Keep An Open Communication

The major objective n any conflict resolution is that both individuals or parties to settle their differences by themselves. You should let the parties to speak out their minds, but also, you must also give them your viewpoint. When you allow them to express their viewpoints freely, it would let them realize where the problem is, and how to resolve it.

Conclusion

As a supervisor, or any other manager responsible for the success of an organization, you will need to be professional enough. You must also act decisively when solving the conflicts. It is always expected that you will be the neutral person, and for that, you should never take sides. It could happen that there is a conflict between a board member an a subordinate staff. Here, you should listen to both sides, and avoid favouritism. When all sides have been served fairly, there is a higher chance of peace being the outcome.

UNIT 6

CREATING TEAMS

Sure, a group of people working on a project can complete it, and will do a fairly reasonable job. But, your work groups are greatly limiting themselves, and putting your company's reputation on the line (in terms of quality work and delivery), if they aren't working as a team. So, how exactly do you get a group of employees to come together and work as a team? Motivation and productivity will increase when your employees support each other and work together; but, building an effective team is a process, and isn't something that will come together in a few days' time. Here are a few steps to get started on building effective teams in the workplace.

Meet with the group –

Step one is meeting with the group. During this sit down meeting, you want to discuss how working as a team will benefit everyone. It will increase productivity, reduce the amount of time it takes to complete tasks, help increase satisfaction within the group, and help increase productivity. During this time,it is also a good idea to ask employees if they have any suggestions as to how to build a better team.

Getting input from those who are actually going to be working together, will help build a cohesive unit, and mesh everyone together. Not only that, but if certain members of the group aren't comfortable with others, this is a good time to air out differences between employees, with managers present. This will allow people to confront one another, and discuss their differences, in order for them to eventually learn how to work together, in order to build a better team, and in order to build a unit that is going to accomplish the desired goals that the company has in mind.

Explain benefits to the company –

You want your group to know the work they produce, will reflect on the company. When it is well done, this will result in benefits to the team as well. Whether it is performance bonuses, extra time off work (at year's end), pay raises, or other benefits in the form of physical or monetary returns, will give more of an incentive for them to work together. Regardless of what the benefits are, if they are aware they will receive them, employees are more likely to work well together. And, when employees are aware of different benefits that will come their way if they reach certain goals, they are going to work harder in order to receive these benefits. So, their hard work is going to benefit the organization, and in the end, it is also going to be beneficial for each of the individual members who are working together as a team.

Develop different goals for the teams –

It is a good idea to set up small teams within the group, and have them meet specific goals. Whether it is completing a report by a certain deadline, increasing sales by a percentage, or any other goal you set, when teams have goals to reach (rather than working aimlessly), they are more willing to work together to attain that goal. Establishing metrics to determine success, and how well the teams gauge against one another, also provides some bonus (friendly) competition, that may further push them to work together.

Determine how goals can be met –

Set up weekly meetings. Redefine jobs within the team. Creating new tasks for different members to complete. Regardless of the different ways you come up with how to reach goals, if each person has a set job to complete, and if you continually find ways to improve workflow, employees will find it easier to work as a team, so they can meet said goals.

Inform them of progress –

Weekly meetings, regular feedback, positive reinforcement, and other manners exist, in which you can keep the team informed as to whether or not they are meeting their goals, and how well they are working together. If they aren't meeting goals, try offering solutions or changes which can be made, in order for them to be met. If they are doing a good job, let them know. If they aren't meeting goals, it is also important to let them know, and make suggestions so changes can be made, and work will be done more efficiently.

Properly pair your team members –

If you have two individuals who don't see eye to eye, or simply can't get on the same page for a particular project, why would you force them to work together? Rather, look for the employees that mesh well together, and the individuals whose skills compliment one another's. Doing this will allow the pairs to work well together, and will allow smaller pairs to work individually, to eventually attain the overall team goal. Not only does pairing people up within the team right result in more efficient workflow, it will also result in a more amicable workplace, and employees will tend to get along better, when they are working with other team members who they feel comfortable around and working with.

Celebrate small goals –

Remember, the end goal is to get them to feel like a team, and want to work together. What better way than to reward them, and celebrate small goals. Hold a small office party when they finish a big project together. Make sure to thank team members for their work (you would be surprised how a thank you goes a long way). Regardless of how small the goal is, reward, celebrate, and thank them for their hard work.

You won't build a team, out of an individual group, in a few day's time, or even a few weeks. But, implementing new steps gradually, and finding ways to implement team tasks into the workplace, will eventually get your employees to work together, and become a more cohesive team unit. Not only will this benefit them, and help improve the workplace attitude, but it also benefits the company, as work is done more efficiently, and employees perform better within their new team roles.

UNIT 7

TEAM STRATEGIES

Do your staff members snap into action or seem to glaze over immediately after you ask them to complete a task or attend a meeting? It may not be a big deal if your employees are not excited about performing their duties, provided that they are still completing all basic tasks. In fact, lackluster staff members can completely drag the entire company down. Truthfully, when the team doesn't really feel motivated to work, absenteeism can rise and productivity can drop.

Generally, their lack of enthusiasm negatively affects the company's bottom line. In the current difficult financial environment where staff members are usually stretched to their limit and layoffs are frequent, it might be difficult to maintain and keep the spirits of your team up and alive. By investing effort and time into bringing your employees together in harmony and ensure that they all feel valued and respected, you could be certain that your team would overcome hard times and help the company grow stronger and more competitive than ever.

Here are some team strategies that can boost morale in the workplace:

1. Give Your Team an Opportunity to Play

For instance, Google is known to be one of the most innovative companies in the world, but employees do not spend all their working time hunched over their computers. In fact, the company is highly renowned for classic perks, such as a video game rooms, ping-pong tables and a rock climbing wall. You don't need to have a climbing wall in your budget, but it's important and necessary for any business to have the same sense of play by buying some board games. In this case, the key is mainly to give your staff members a chance to take a short break during working hours to build mutual friendships and de-stress.

2. Don't Overwork Your Employees

It's also important to make sure that your team is not being overworked and are maintaining a better work-life balance. Simply start by setting a good, positive example yourself. For instance, as a manager, by skipping an important family matter to deal with a client emergency, you're sending a clear message that work is actually important than your family. This can be a surefire way of damaging morale and losing top talent. Additionally, it's a good idea to take note of who is really overworking and to help them identify ways of cutting back their time in the workplace. Even if you consider hiring new people, it could be well worth the expense to keep a key staff member motivated and also to prevent staff turnover.

3. Organize For Team Events of Out-Of-Office

When there is friction, especially in the workplace, a day together as a team aware from the office could help relax the team's tension and improve the general mood. When planning any excursion, consider activities that would help encourage everyone to work together as a team, to achieve a common goal. For example, you decide to engage your employees in building structures or to participate in a paintball game, just for a day. When planning such events, it's important to keep the fitness level and health of your staff members in mind. Then, ensure that you have organized an activity that everyone would be capable of participating in.

4. Offer Free Coffee, Snacks and Meals

In this hard economic times, several companies have actually decided to cut back on some expenses such as free office snacks. It is a bad decision because nothing is more likely to kill the employees' morale knowing that he/she cannot even count on his/her tea break or free morning coffee anymore. Instead, choose the opposite direction and make sure that your team always gets high-quality food or drinks. This will make and keep staff members happy in the workplace.

5. Advocate for Your Team

When a client or customer is mistreating or deliberately insulting one of your staff members, it's your responsibility to stand up for your employee. Occasionally, clients can treat an individual member of your team with blatant disrespect. If that happens, standing up for them in a respectful and professional way, even if it means losing a potential business deal, shows how much you really care about your employees. Eventually, chances are that the team is going to be more worthy to you than any belligerent customer or client.

6. Give Your Team More Insight on How the Company Operates.

Giving your employees more input, especially into how the whole company runs is also important. Employees usually become easily disengaged if they feel that their opinions don't really matter at all. In order to counteract such attitude, ensure that everyone has an opportunity to give suggestions or express their opinions on issues regarding the workplace, especially concerning working conditions. It's possible to find some useful ideas on how work to operate more efficiently.

It's also important to give your employees some autonomy to establish and implement ideas within their control. Similarly, you can ask your team for opinions or suggestions on how to resolve a problem. Basically, involvement results in an engagement and this can help the staff members feel included and important.

7. Give Credit for Work Well Done

Staff members can in fact become fed-up with their duties and responsibilities when they feel or think their work is not being recognized by their mangers or supervisors. Therefore, be sure to track the progress of every employee and try to recognize anyone that comes up with a better or more innovative solution to an issue or someone who has surpassed a goal.

Conclusively, company awards programs can also serve as a very powerful way of commending your team for making an impact on the company. Consider giving monthly employee awards where winners would get gift certificates, as well as other prizes. Lastly, open communication, a sense of play and respect are all essential hallmarks of a healthy and happy workplace. You can easily transform your workplace by simply following these useful steps and you will see the dedication levels of your employees rise, together with the company's bottom line.

UNIT 8

TIME MANAGEMENT

Time management is among the most vital aspects that will determine the success of an organization. Teams and supervisors in an organization are expected to greatly observe the time management. Time is a tool that will determine if a given project would be completed as expected. Everything that goes on in the organization is carried out on the basis of the time. With time management, it involves the setting of goals, and organizing how they would be achieved. Unless the supervisor and teams have the right time management skills, there would be a lot of time wasted.

It requires one to be disciplined in managing their time, in order to be able to accomplish the set goals. Basically, time management is important, both to the teams and the supervisors in an organization. *Time management in an organization is important for the following reasons:*

• It Enhances Prioritization

With the right time management in an organization, the supervisors will be able to prioritize the activities and projects, for the sake of the business' success. The management of time will help the supervisors and teams to rank the activities and project in order of their relevance. This can be observed daily, for the sake of ensuring that the project is progressing.

• Goals Setting

When you are considering time management, you should set long term and short term goals and then set deadlines. These could be adjusted as necessary.

• Increased Productivity

Time management also greatly contributes towards increased productivity. The supervisors and the teams would put more focus on the projects, along with their timelines. As a result, there would be a more efficient way of completing tasks.

• Increased Performance

The performance of the teams would also be increased majorly when there is a deep observance of time. Since the productivity would be increased, the performance would also be increased. With proper time management, one will be able to get on another project, even ahead of time.

• Eliminates Procrastination

Delay is a major enemy of time management. There could be a number of employees in the organization, who are fond of postponing their tasks. With an effective time management plan, every person would know their role, and the time limit. With the observation of the time, the employees would make sure that they have completed their roles within the time frame. If there is no specific time frame defined for a certain role, the teams would ignore them, and postpone them. Basically, the time management helps in reminding the employees that their work should be completed by a certain time or date.

• Helps To Nurture The Employees

If a particular task is set to be carried out by a certain employee within a given period of time, it would help to develop them. If a given project is successfully completed by one employee, on the basis of the time management, the supervisor could apply it to another employee. This would help employees learn how to complete their tasks within a shorter period of time.

• Helps To Monitor The Employees

There are software that are used by supervisors to manage the organizational operations. These software can track down the activities of employees, in relation to their time management. It could monitor employees' arrivals in the morning, lunch breaks, day break, or even offs and monthly leaves. With the right time management software, you would be able to know the behavior of your employees.

• Gets Rid Of Bad Behaviors

Since the time management software help supervisors to track down the habits of the employees, this would discourage them from being lazy and missing work. Also, the supervisor can implement sanctions in cases where an employee does not complete assigned task on time. This would generally discourage the employees from developing bad habits. Even though it might take some time to completely eradicate the bad habit, it would eventually be possible.

• It Motivates The Team

Another importance of time management is that it helps to motivate the team. For instance, the supervisor can give the team incentives for finishing their work ahead of time. There could be special gifts that could be designed for the successful completion of a task. Also, the team would be motivated to work harder, in order to complete more tasks ahead of time.

• Allows Time For Resting

Laziness is an enemy to the progress of an organization, but also, too much work can be very dangerous to the employees. That is why they should be encouraged to have enough rest, for the sake of refreshing the mind. If time management is carried out successfully, it would help a person to complete their job in time, and have enough time to rest. An effective time management gives the team more time to rest.

Conclusion

Generally, time management helps the team and the supervisors to be sure of a successful project. Mostly, it is all about achieving the set objectives within the time frame. This is mostly what will determine the success of a project. The results would come later, but what matters most is being able to complete tasks on time.